About the Book

The features of *Grammar and Punctuation, Grade 2* include:

25 Rule Charts

Reproduce these charts on overhead transparencies for ease of presentation.

Choose the rules and the order of use that are appropriate to the needs of your students.

Review the charts regularly.

3 Practice Pages for Each Rule

Use as many reproducible practice pages as appropriate for your students. These pages may be used with the whole class or as independent practice. You may wish to do a single practice page each time you review a rule.

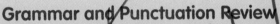

Grammar and Punctuation Review

This four-page review provides a means of evaluating your students' acquisition of the grammar and punctuation skills presented. With young students, you may wish to use the review pages one at a time, perhaps using the entire review again at year-end.

Student Record Sheet

On the student record sheet, the grammar and punctuation skills are keyed to the practice pages and test items.

Answer Key

A complete answer key begins on page 108.

About the CD-ROM

Loading the Program

1

Put the CD in your CD drive. This CD-ROM contains both Windows and MacOS programs.

Your computer will recognize the correct program.

2

On some computers, the program will automatically start up. If the program does not start automatically:

Windows—go to *My Computer*, double click on the CD drive, then double click on *Begin.exe*.

MacOS—double click on the CD icon on your desktop, then double click on *Begin*.

3

After the program starts, you will arrive at the main menu.

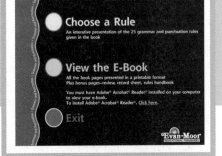

Main Menu Features

⬤ Choose a Rule

It's never been more fun to practice grammar and punctuation! The 25 rule charts found in the book are presented in full-color with an interactive element. To present a whole-class lesson, connect your computer to a projection system. As a review, students may be instructed on how to access specific rule charts during their computer time.

1
Click the *Choose a Rule* button to display the list of rules.

2
Click on a rule in the list of rules. The rule will be displayed.

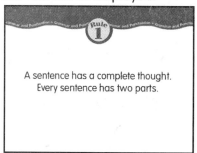

3
Click on the arrow button.

Rule explanations and examples will be displayed.

4
When you're finished, click on **List of Rules** ⬤ to go back to the rules list or click on ⬤ **Main Menu** to go back to the main menu.

⬤ View the E-Book

- The rule charts, practice pages, and answer key are presented in a printable electronic format. You must have Adobe® Acrobat® Reader™ installed to access the e-book. (See installation instructions in sidebar.)

- You may scroll through the entire book page by page or open the "Bookmarks" tab for a clickable table of contents.

  > **Hint:** This symbol, + for Windows or ▷ for MacOS, means that you can click there to expand this category.

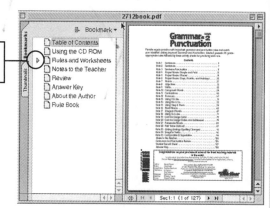

- To print pages from the e-book, click on the printer icon. A print dialog box will open. Enter the page or pages you wish to print in the print range boxes. (At the bottom of the screen, you can see which page of the e-book you are viewing.)

- To exit the e-box, simply "X" out until you return to the main menu.

E-Book Bonus
Also on the e-book is a reproducible rules handbook for students. Each rule is shown with room for students to write their own examples of the rule.

⬤ Exit
This button closes the program.

Installing Adobe® Acrobat® Reader™
You need to have Acrobat Reader installed on your computer to access the e-book portion of the CD-ROM. If you do not have Acrobat Reader, go to the main menu of the CD and follow these instructions:

1. Place your cursor over the *Click Here* link. Wait for the hand and then click.

2. When you see the Acrobat Reader Setup Screen, click the "Next" box.

3. When you see the Destination Location Screen, click the "Next" box.

4. When you see the Setup Complete Screen, click "finish."

Your system will now shut down in order to install Acrobat Reader. Some systems will automatically restart. If yours does not, start it up manually.

Rule 1

A sentence has a complete thought.
Every sentence has two parts.

- It names something or someone.

- It tells what that something or someone is or does.*

The dog runs fast.

Ann hit the ball.

That boy is happy.

*See Notes to the Teacher on page 103 for additional information.

Sentences

What Is a Sentence?

Circle the sentences. Put a line through the groups of words that are not sentences.

(Tom and Julie played ball.)

~~The flower pot.~~

1. Climbed the mountain and camped.

2. The class went to the library.

3. Marilyn ate her lunch.

4. Susan, Bill, and Jack.

5. The flag waved in the wind.

6. The cute little puppy.

7. Sat down on the bench.

Parts of a Sentence

Circle the part of the sentence that names something or someone. Underline the part of the sentence that tells what that something or someone does.

(Tom) raced down the street.

1. Nick rode his new blue bike.

2. Susie and Toshi played with the dollhouse.

3. The two girls jumped up and down.

4. Becky and her grandmother played in the snow.

5. Jonathan flew his paper airplane.

6. Mrs. Smith's class walked to the lunchroom.

7. Each boy read two books.

8. Isabel won the race.

9. Mom and Dad went to the store.

Put It Together

Cut and group.

talks
walks
works

Names something or someone

paste
paste
paste

Tells what it is or does

paste
paste
paste

---

rode their bikes.	Jane and Tamara	raced down the street.
Two big dogs	played checkers.	Cindy and Daniel

Rule 2

A sentence begins with a capital letter.

All the children walked down the hall.

Spot hid a bone in the garden.

There are two birds in the nest.

Sentences

Begin with a Capital Letter

A Fix this story. Begin each complete sentence with a capital letter.

T

1. the mother bird wanted to make a nest.

2. flew over trees and a barn.

3. then she came to a big white house.

4. there was a porch on one side.

5. inside the porch.

6. there was a little ledge.

7. high enough to be safe.

8. the bird started gathering straw and sticks.

B Write a sentence that tells what happened next in the story. Be sure to begin your sentence with a capital letter.

_____

_____

Name _____

Guess My Pet

A Write these sentences. Begin each sentence with a capital letter.

1. my pet lives in a cage.

_____

2. it can talk and squawk.

_____

3. my pet has a beak.

_____

4. it has green and yellow feathers.

_____

B Draw a picture of my pet.

Name _____

Start with a Capital Letter

Circle the letter that should begin each sentence.

1. ☐ I i ☐ love to read books.

2. ☐ I i ☐ t is fun to read with my friends.

3. ☐ m M ☐ y friend, Ryan, likes to read books about cars.

4. ☐ s S ☐ arah enjoys art books.

5. ☐ E e ☐ lizabeth loves books about animals.

6. ☐ m M ☐ olly thinks fairy tales are wonderful.

7. ☐ S s ☐ cience books are my favorites.

8. ☐ w W ☐ e read our books together every day.

A sentence needs end punctuation.

- A **telling sentence** ends with a **period** (.).

    The dogs barked when the doorbell rang**.**

    Sally danced across the floor like a butterfly**.**

- An **asking sentence** ends with a **question mark** (**?**).

    Where did you go**?**

    Does a mouse eat cheese**?**

- A sentence that shows strong feeling ends with an **exclamation mark** (**!**).

    Help, I'm falling**!**

    Don't touch that stove**!**

Sentence Punctuation

Asks or Tells?

Cut and group.

Period (.)	**Question Mark (?)**
paste	paste
paste	paste
paste	paste

✂ -

Pizza is my favorite food	What is your favorite kind	Do you like pepperoni on it
I like a lot of cheese on mine	Which toppings do you like	Many toppings can go on a pizza

Exclamation Marks

Read each group of words. Cross out the groups of words that are **not** sentences. Write the correct punctuation mark at the end of sentences. Use **.**, **?**, or **!**.

1. Juan and Maria put up the tent

2. Hurry, Maria, a storm is coming

3. They finished just before the rain started

4. Raindrops, raindrops, raindrops

5. Juan, will the tent keep us safe

6. Hooray, the rain is stopping

7. Juan and Maria smiled at the rainbow

13

The End

Write a period (.), a question mark (?), or an exclamation mark (!) in each box.

1. Do you know what I did last week ☐

2. Our family went to the Children's Museum ☐

3. Wow, did we have fun ☐

4. We did a science experiment in the lab ☐

5. I put some things in a test tube ☐

6. My dad put the test tube over a flame ☐

7. Can you guess what happened ☐

8. Pop ☐

9. Boy, my mom was surprised ☐

10. Have you ever been to the Children's Museum ☐

     Grammar and Punctuation, Grade 2 • EMC 2712

The names of people and pets begin with capital letters.

Bill and **Pat** like to fish.

Mr. Lee is my neighbor.

Our teacher, **Ms. Lopez**, has a cat named **Tippy**.

My dog, **Sandy**, likes to run through the sprinkler.

Proper Nouns

Names of People and Pets

Fix the sentences. Begin each name with a capital letter.

1. mark had two pets.

2. One was a black cat named midnight.

3. The other was a frisky puppy named baby.

4. baby liked to chase midnight.

5. One day midnight jumped up on the fence.

6. baby could not reach midnight.

7. The fence was too high.

8. Then baby jumped into the flower box and stood on his hind legs.

9. But midnight was still too high!

Name _____

What's Your Name?

Write names to answer these questions. Begin each name with a capital letter.

1. What is your name? _____

2. What is your friend's name? _____

3. What is your teacher's name? _____

4. Who is tall? _____

5. Who is funny? _____

6. Who sits next to you? _____

7. Who loves to read? _____

8. Who loves recess? _____

Write That Name

Write these sentences. Begin each name with a capital letter.

1. kristen played checkers with ronnie.

_____

2. My dog, socks, likes to chase balls.

_____

3. mrs. gonzalez told us a funny story.

_____

4. My dentist, dr. hopkins, checked my teeth.

_____

5. karl took rover for a walk.

_____

6. Our principal, mr. lee, read us a story.

_____

The names of specific places begin with capital letters.

Hillside Park is a good place for a walk.

I live in **Eaton, Colorado**.

Bayview School sits high on a hill.

Disneyland is my favorite amusement park.

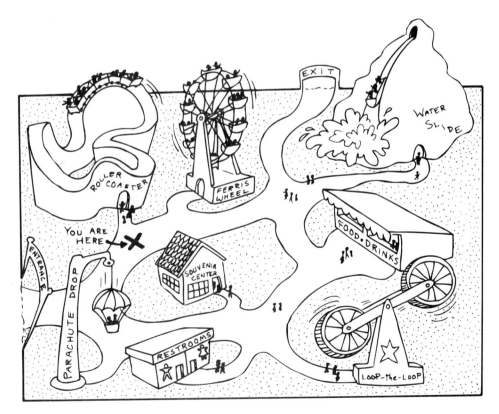

Proper Nouns

Names of Places

A Fix the sentences. Begin the names of people, pets, and specific places with capital letters.

1. In rocky mountain national park, snow stays on the mountains in the summer.

2. I hiked around a lake with my sister, colby.

3. sweet pea and blossom, our dogs, had to wear their leashes.

4. Tomorrow we will go to denver to see a ball game.

5. My friend, leonard, found a dog when he was at sunset beach.

B Write about a place that you have visited. Remember to use capital letters.

_____

_____

_____

Name _____

Name That Place

Write answers to these questions. Begin the names of specific places with capital letters.

1. What is the name of your school?

_____

2. What city do you live in?

_____

3. What state do you live in?

_____

4. What is your favorite amusement park?

_____

5. What is your favorite restaurant?

_____

6. What is one place you would like to visit?

_____

21

On the Road

Write these names of places. Remember to begin the names of specific places with capital letters.

1. disneyland _____

2. los angeles _____

3. yosemite national park _____

4. mount rushmore _____

5. colonial williamsburg _____

6. carlsbad caverns _____

7. mississippi river _____

8. cape cod _____

The names of the days of the week, months of the year, and holidays begin with capital letters.

Days	I go to dance class on **Wednesday**. On **Tuesday** and **Thursday** I play soccer.
Months	**January** is the first month of the year. My birthday is in **July**.
Holidays	**Independence Day** is a special celebration. **Kwanzaa** lasts for seven days.

July

S	M	T	W	Th	F	S
1	2	3	4	5	6	7
8	9	10	11	12	13	14
15	16	17	18	19	20	21
22	23	24	25	26	27	28
29	30	31				

Proper Nouns

Names of Days

A Read the sentences. Write the name of each day of the week. Begin with a capital letter.

1. I can't wait to go to school on monday. _____

2. wednesday is my sharing day. _____

3. On friday we will go on a field trip. _____

4. The cooks fixed a special treat on tuesday. _____

5. My family drove to the beach on sunday. _____

6. Our soccer team plays on saturday. _____

B What is your favorite day of the week? Write a sentence that tells why.

My favorite day of the week is _____

because _____

_____.

Names of Months

Begin the names of the months with capital letters.

The first month is ____anuary. Next comes

____ebruary, the month for valentines. The third

month is ____arch, the time for leprechauns. Next

comes ____pril, then ____ay and ____une. ____uly

is the month for fireworks.

The eighth month is ____ugust. School often begins

in the month of ____eptember. The month for pumpkins

is called ____ctober. In ____ovember we give thanks.

The last month is ____ecember.

Names of Holidays

Fix the sentences. Capitalize the names of holidays. Capitalize any other words that should begin with a capital letter.

1. we plan to watch the fireworks on independence day.

2. the class drew leprechauns for st. patrick's day.

3. michael's birthday is on father's day this year.

4. did you hunt for eggs on easter?

5. mrs. smith's class learned about chinese new year.

6. tenisha's family had a party during kwanzaa.

7. we roasted a big turkey for thanksgiving.

8. did you make mother a card for valentine's day?

Rule 7

A noun is a word that names a person, place, or thing.

person	place	thing
boy	school	cat
teacher	beach	truck
baby	town	cloud
player	store	carrot

place

person

thing

Nouns

Find the Nouns

A Circle the nouns in this story. Can you find all 16?

Zip lay down under the tree. A little bee buzzed near

his ear. Zip flipped his tail at the bee and rolled over in

the grass. It was a quiet day. The family had gone to the

beach. The house was empty. The sun was warm. Zip

yawned. Soon Zip was dreaming of a yummy bone.

B Now write a sentence that tells what Zip is.

_____

_____

Name That Noun

Rule 7

A Write each noun under the correct heading.

school	teacher	book
jump rope	pencil	playground
girl	library	boy

person	place	thing
_____	_____	_____
_____	_____	_____
_____	_____	_____

B Write a noun in each blank.

1. _____ went to _____ to buy _____.
   person   place   thing

2. _____ played with _____ at _____.
   person   thing   place

3. Did _____ eat _____ at _____?
   person   thing   place

Draw a Noun

A Draw a picture of a person, a place, and a thing. Write the name of each noun on the line.

1. person	2. place	3. thing

_____   _____   _____

B Write a sentence using each noun.

1. _____

2. _____

3. _____

Rule 8

Some words describe nouns.
These words are called adjectives.

pretty flower   **round** ball   **huge** giant

wet towel   **tall** tree   **tiny** baby

hot soup   **dark** night   **blue** bike

Adjectives

Words That Describe

A Circle the adjectives in the sentences below.

1. The fluffy yellow kitten sat by the round bowl.

2. Its big green eyes blinked.

3. It watched the tiny silver fish swim in the clear water.

4. It tilted its head and lifted a flat, white paw.

5. The fish darted into some green, leafy plants.

6. The kitten went off to play with its gray toy mouse.

B Write an adjective in each blank.

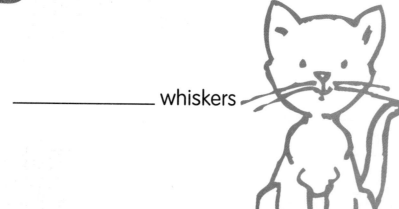

_____ ears

_____ whiskers

_____ tail

Name _____

Add an Adjective

Write an adjective to tell **how many** or **what kind** in the blanks.

1. A _____ car zoomed down the street.

2. We saw _____ dinosaurs at the museum.

3. A _____ girl helped me with my homework.

4. The _____ clown made the children smile.

5. _____ boys played a game of basketball.

6. The _____ boats sailed down the _____ river.

7. The _____ seagulls flew over the _____ ocean.

8. A _____ lizard ran across the _____ sand.

9. The _____ ball rolled down the _____ hill.

10. A _____ mouse ate a _____ piece of cheese.

How Many Adjectives?

Circle the adjectives. Fill in the circle that tells how many adjectives you found in each sentence.

1. My dad and I went to see a funny movie last night. ① ② ③

2. There were lots of fast cars and quick boats. ① ② ③

3. The story was about two silly men. ① ② ③

4. They wore big, funny, colorful hats. ① ② ③

5. One of them wore large red shoes. ① ② ③

6. One wore a gigantic yellow tie. ① ② ③

7. The silly men were trying to find a loud green bird. ① ② ③

8. In the end, the quick bird got away. ① ② ③

Verbs are words that tell what is happening or what already happened. They name an action.

what is happening	what already happened
sit	smiled
swing	frowned
sleep	climbed
dig	hiked
run	played
eat	grew
talk	picked

Verbs

Find the Verbs

Read the sentences. Draw a line under the verbs. The first one has been done for you.

1. Shane planted the little seed.

2. The sun warmed the brown earth.

3. The rain watered the seed.

4. A tiny green sprout poked its head above the ground.

5. The sprout grew and grew.

6. Soon the sprout was a tall, slim cornstalk.

7. Ears of corn appeared on the stalk.

8. Shane picked the ears in August.

9. He ate lots of yummy corn on the cob.

Add a Verb

Read the sentences. Complete the sentences by adding a verb.

1. The puppies _____ with the ball.

2. The boys _____ down the street.

3. The ball _____ up and down.

4. We _____ with the jump rope.

5. We _____ when we play hopscotch.

6. She _____ her bike to my house.

7. He _____ the ball to his friend.

8. Our kite _____ in the sky.

Name _____

Draw a Verb

A Draw a picture of an action (a verb) in each box. Write the verb on the line.

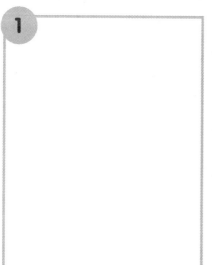

_____ _____ _____

B Write a sentence using each verb.

1. _____

2. _____

3. _____

Two words can sometimes be put together to make a new word. The new word is called a compound word.

butter + fly = **butterfly**

pop + corn = **popcorn**

door + bell = **doorbell**

foot + ball = **football**

in + side = **inside**

Compound Words

Grammar and Punctuation, Grade 2 • EMC 2712

Find the Compound Words

Circle the compound word in each sentence. Write the two words that make the compound word.

1. He opened the mailbox and took out the mail.

   _____   _____

2. The children played in the sandbox.

   _____   _____

3. Our class loves to play baseball.

   _____   _____

4. We collected seashells as we walked along the beach.

   _____   _____

5. At recess we play games on the playground.

   _____   _____

Make Compound Words

Rule 10

Cut out the words. Put them together to make compound words. Paste the compound words onto another sheet of paper.

down	ball
note	book
in	knob
base	lace
shoe	to
door	hill

Draw the Compound Words

Write each compound word. Draw a picture of each compound word.

1.  = _____

2.  = _____

3.  = _____

4. 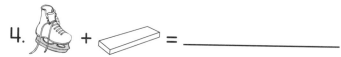 = _____

5.  = _____

6.  = _____

Rule 11

A contraction is a short way to write two words.
A contraction uses an apostrophe (').

cannot = **can't**

is not = **isn't**

could not = **couldn't**

will not = **won't**

it is = **it's**

they will = **they'll**

they are = **they're**

I have = **I've**

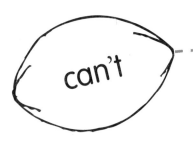

Contractions

Name _____

Learn About Contractions

A Write the letter or letters that are missing in each contraction.

1. do + not = don't   _____

2. I + would = I'd   _____

3. could + not = couldn't _____

4. it + is = it's   _____

5. I + will = I'll   _____

6. they + are = they're   _____

7. have + not = haven't   _____

8. I + have = I've   _____

B Write sentences using two of the contractions above.

1. _____

_____

2. _____

_____

Contractions with Not

Rule 11

Write the correct contraction on each line.

haven't	doesn't	isn't	couldn't	didn't
can't	aren't	weren't	don't	wouldn't

1. have not _____

2. do not _____

3. would not _____

4. is not _____

5. did not _____

6. could not _____

7. were not _____

8. are not _____

9. can not _____

10. does not _____

Write the Contractions

A Write the contraction.

1. you are _____

2. we are _____

3. he is _____

4. I would _____

5. that is _____

6. she is _____

7. it is _____

8. I will _____

9. I am _____

10. let us _____

B Make a match.

I am	I'll
has not	haven't
are not	she'll
she will	hasn't
have not	aren't
I will	she's
she is	I'm

Some words take the place of names (nouns). These words are called pronouns.

one person or thing	more than one person or thing
she	we
her	us
he	they
him	them
it	

Cindy rode a bike. **She** just learned how to stop.

Pablo practiced running. **He** won the race.

Mr. Kwan's class is going on a field trip.
They will take lunches with **them**.

My pet hen found a worm. **She** will eat **it**.

Pronouns

Which Pronoun?

Rewrite each sentence using a pronoun to replace the underlined name.

1. <u>Harry</u> hit a home run.

_____

2. <u>Mrs. Smith</u> drives a school bus.

_____

3. I couldn't wait to see the <u>Empire State Building</u>.

_____

4. I invited <u>Doug</u> to my birthday party.

_____

5. <u>Trina</u> waved to <u>Matt</u> from the bus.

_____

6. <u>The whale</u> was the biggest thing <u>Roy</u> had ever seen.

_____

     Grammar and Punctuation, Grade 2 • EMC 2712

Name _____

Add a Pronoun

Add pronouns to complete the story.

Donna and I are good friends. _____ love to

play games and read books. _____ like to play checkers

and dominoes. _____ are terrific games to play. When

_____ are outside, _____ like to play soccer or

baseball. Donna is a good kicker, but _____ am a great

hitter. _____ also love to read books. <u>Charlotte's Web</u>

is my favorite. _____ is a wonderful story. Donna likes

_____, too.

Nouns and Pronouns

Write pronouns on the lines to replace the circled words.

1. Some (snow) is falling. _____ is falling.

2. (Steve and I) want to play outside. _____ want to play outside.

3. (Steve) put on his snowsuit. _____ put on his snowsuit.

4. My (mom) put on some boots. _____ put on some boots.

5. (Uncle Ralph) grabbed his jacket. _____ grabbed his jacket.

6. (Dad and Mom) got out the sled. _____ got out the sled.

7. (Steve and I) dashed outside. _____ dashed outside.

8. The (snow) was terrific! _____ was terrific!

Use **I** when you are the person doing something.
Use **me** when something happens to you.

I read a book.

I climbed a tree.

I chased the ball.

A dog barked at **me**.

My friend sent a letter to **me**.

Bobby gave **me** some candy.

Using I & Me

I or Me?

Write **I** or **me** to complete the sentences.

1. _____ want to go to Andrew's birthday party.

2. Andrew gave _____ an invitation.

3. Michael and _____ will go together.

4. _____ will wear my swimsuit.

5. My friends and _____ will bring our beach towels and squirt guns.

6. Andrew asked _____ to be on his team.

7. Some friends on the other team will squirt _____.

8. Then _____ will squirt them!

Name _____

Which One?

Fill in the circle that tells the correct pronoun for each blank.

1. When ___ grow up, I want to be a fire fighter.   ○ **I**   ○ **me**

2. Bob gave the ball to ___.   ○ **I**   ○ **me**

3. Jim and ___ played in the park.   ○ **I**   ○ **me**

4. Taylor and Amy gave ___ a doll for my birthday.   ○ **I**   ○ **me**

5. Mrs. Johnson asked ___ to read the story.   ○ **I**   ○ **me**

6. ___ saw a movie on Saturday afternoon.   ○ **I**   ○ **me**

7. The librarian gave the book to ___.   ○ **I**   ○ **me**

8. Jesse and ___ love to play soccer.   ○ **I**   ○ **me**

53 Grammar and Punctuation, Grade 2 • EMC 2712

Choose I or Me

Cut and group.

You are doing something

paste
paste
paste

Something happens to you

paste
paste
paste

✂ --

I like to play baseball.	Please give me the ball.	Kelly handed me the paper.
Sam and I are reading.	Marta worked with me.	I went to the store.

         Grammar and Punctuation, Grade 2 • EMC 2712

Use **we** when you and other people do something. Use **us** when something happens to you and other people.

We went to the store.

We ran a race.

We ate ice cream.

The police officer helped **us**.

My mom asked **us** to baby-sit.

Is that cake for **us** to eat?

Using We & Us

Name _____

We or Us?

Answer the questions. Use **we** or **us**.

1. What do you and your friends like to do?

_____

2. What do you and your friends like to eat?

_____

3. What does the coach expect your team to do during practice?

_____

4. What did your teacher tell your class when you went out for recess?

_____

5. What did you and your family do last Saturday?

_____

Name _____

Which One?

Fill in the circle that tells the correct pronoun for each blank.

1. ___ like to go looking for bugs.   ○ **We**   ○ **Us**

2. My teacher gave ___ some paper.   ○ **we**   ○ **us**

3. Donnie threw the ball to ___.   ○ **we**   ○ **us**

4. On the field trip ___ saw interesting rocks.   ○ **we**   ○ **us**

5. ___ bought a birthday present for Tom.   ○ **We**   ○ **Us**

6. Our principal gave ___ awards for good work.   ○ **we**   ○ **us**

7. The clerk handed ___ the package.   ○ **we**   ○ **us**

8. ___ played on the swings at the park.   ○ **We**   ○ **Us**

Name _____

Choose Us or We

Cut and group.

You and others do something

paste
paste
paste

Something happens to you and others

paste
paste
paste

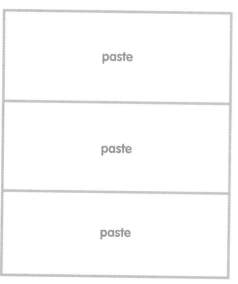

We went to the playground.	Mom gave us some drinks.	Dad took us to the game.
We played basketball.	Carla read a book to us.	At school we learn new things.

Use **they** when several people do something.
Use **them** when something happens to
several people.

They built a house.

They helped fix my bike.

They solved the problem.

Mr. Brown asked **them** to stand up.

The mayor gave **them** an award.

Do you go to school with **them**?

They are singing. m m m m m m

Using They & Them

Use the Word They

Rewrite each sentence using **they** for the underlined names.

1. Frank and Robert take cooking lessons.

_____

2. Yesterday Janice and Jose joined the class.

_____

3. Frank, Robert, Janice, and Jose made a fruit salad.

_____

4. Then Robert and Janice ate it.

_____

5. Frank and Jose washed the dishes.

_____

Write They or Them

Read the stories. Fill in the blanks with the pronouns **they** or **them**.

Tony, Elise, and Sam wanted to plan a class party.

_____ asked Mrs. Supino for permission. Mrs. Supino told

_____ that it was okay. _____ planned games and

made snacks. The class loved it. All of the students thanked

_____ for planning the party.

Last month Robin's dog had puppies. _____

were so tiny. The mother dog took good care of _____.

Now _____ are running around. Robin likes to play

with _____. Then _____ fall asleep on her lap.

_____ are so cute!

Choose They or Them

Cut and group.

Several people do something

paste
paste
paste

Something happens to several people

paste
paste
paste

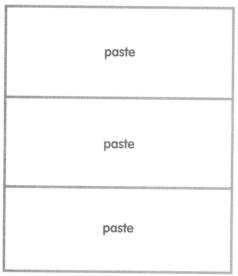

Chaz asked them to help.	They played with Tina.	Jamal worked with them.
Later they went to the park.	They ran to the swings.	Pedro tossed the ball to them.

Add **s** or **es** to name more than one.

- Add **s** to most nouns to name more than one.

  one shoe—two shoe**s**   one apple—two apple**s**

  one snake—two snake**s**   one girl—two girl**s**

- Add **es** to some nouns ending in **ch**, **x**, **sh**, or **z** to name more than one.

  one dish—two dish**es**   one bus—two bus**es**

  one bench—two bench**es**   one box—two box**es**

bus   buses

Plural Nouns

More Than One

Circle the word that completes each sentence.

1. I put on both of my _____.   shoe   shoes

2. Bob wore a _____.   hats   hat

3. I hear a barking _____.   dog   dogs

4. She put a ball in the _____.   boxes   box

5. He rode his _____.   bike   bikes

6. We're on her _____.   teams   team

7. We need two _____.   dish   dishes

8. Our school has three _____.   buses   bus

shoe

shoes

Count the Syllables

Write the number of syllables for each base word. Add **s** or **es** to each word to make it mean **more than one**. Then write the number of syllables for the new word.

Base Word	Syllables	Add s or es	Syllables
brush	1	brushes	2
1. stamp	_____	_____	_____
2. dish	_____	_____	_____
3. dog	_____	_____	_____
4. sandwich	_____	_____	_____
5. cupcake	_____	_____	_____
6. bench	_____	_____	_____
7. frog	_____	_____	_____
8. fox	_____	_____	_____

Counting syllables can help you know if you add **s** or **es**.

More Than One

Add **s** or **es** to make these words plural.

1. two book   _____

2. four pencil   _____

3. three paintbrush   _____

4. two new desk   _____

5. four paper   _____

6. five sandwich   _____

7. two milk   _____

8. six peach   _____

9. three board game   _____

10. four puzzle   _____

11. lots of building block   _____

12. one box of checker   _____

          Grammar and Punctuation, Grade 2 • EMC 2712

Some special nouns mean more than one.

one	more than one
tooth	teeth
mouse	mice
child	children
man	men
foot	feet
goose	geese
woman	women

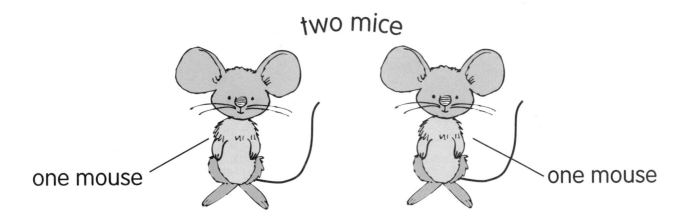

two mice

one mouse

one mouse

Irregular Plurals

Special More-Than-One Nouns

Label each picture with a word from the Word Box. Then choose the correct word to complete each sentence.

_____   _____   _____

_____   _____   _____

1. Some _____ made a nest in the old clothes bag.

2. Only one _____ at a time may leave the room.

3. Three _____ drove to work together.

4. Did all the _____ finish their homework?

Word Box

| mouse | mice | man | men | child | children |

Make a Match

Draw a line to match the pictures to the words.

foot

teeth

goose

feet

tooth

child

geese

children

Grammar and Punctuation, Grade 2 • EMC 2712

More Special Words

Rule 17

Use words from the box to complete the sentences.

1. A _____ played on the swings.

2. A _____ swam across the lake.

3. She lost her first _____.

4. He put his shoes on his _____.

5. The _____ played tag in the field.

6. The _____ all wore red dresses.

7. The _____ flew in a V-shaped pattern.

8. She put one sock on her _____.

9. Be sure to brush your _____.

10. Look at that _____ in the pink dress!

Word Box

child	children	goose	geese	tooth
teeth	foot	feet	woman	women

Rule 18

Use **is** with one. Use **are** with more than one.

The boy **is** climbing the ladder.

The boys **are** climbing the ladder.

She **is** my best friend.

They **are** my best friends.

A bird **is** sitting on the wire.

Some birds **are** sitting on the wire.

She is

We are

Using Is & Are

Use Is and Are

Read the sentences. Write **is** or **are** in the blanks.

1. Two birds _____ outside my window.

2. They _____ building a nest.

3. The nest _____ up in a tall tree.

4. The mother bird _____ looking for dry grass.

5. She _____ flying all around.

6. The father bird _____ searching for small twigs.

7. He _____ hopping on the ground.

8. They _____ very busy.

9. When the nest is finished, they _____ going to have a family.

10. I will watch the baby birds as they _____ hatching.

Is or Are?

Circle **is** or **are** to complete the sentences.

1. My bike (is are) red.

2. My brother's bike (is are) blue.

3. Our bikes (is are) very fast.

4. They (is are) 10-speed bikes.

5. My bike (is are) best for racing.

6. My brother's bike (is are) best for rough roads.

7. LaToya's bike (is are) a 5-speed bike.

8. It (is are) a pink and silver beauty!

9. Jill and Steve (is are) good riders.

10. They (is are) very careful when they ride.

Fill in the Circle

Fill in the circle to complete the sentences.

1. We ___ building an airplane. ○ is ○ are

2. Janna ___ cutting the wood. ○ is ○ are

3. Jim and Bob ___ measuring the wings. ○ is ○ are

4. Cathy ___ trimming the rudder. ○ is ○ are

5. Jonathan ___ assembling the body. ○ is ○ are

6. Elliot and Matt ___ cutting the covering. ○ is ○ are

7. Chris ___ attaching the rubber band. ○ is ○ are

8. Denise ___ fixing the propeller. ○ is ○ are

What are we going to do when we finish building the airplane?

_____

Use commas (,) to separate things in a list.

Margo has cats, dogs, and fish for pets.

Are you wearing gloves, boots, and a sweater today?

I bought chocolate milk, vanilla ice cream, and peanut butter at the store.

Comma Usage

Add the Commas

Add commas in the sentences to separate three or more things in a list.

1. He bought nails screws and wood to build his doghouse.

2. We bought oranges apples pears and bananas at the grocery store.

3. Mike asked Tory Cassie Jake Jared and Jesse to the party.

4. I have sheets blankets and a bedspread on my bed.

5. We took books games magazines and puzzles on our trip.

6. The Scouts will need backpacks sleeping bags clothes and food for camp.

7. We used pink purple and silver paint in LaDonna's bedroom.

8. My favorite sandwich has peanut butter honey and bananas on it.

What does your favorite sandwich have on it?

_____

_____

Words in a List

Write a sentence using each word list. Use commas to separate the items.

raincoat
compass
flashlight
water bottle

1. Tell what Tom packed for his camping trip.

_____

_____

peach yogurt
string cheese
carrots
chocolate milk

2. Tell what Jolynn had in her lunch.

_____

_____

Thomas
Chris
Todd
Lee

3. Tell who Andrew is inviting to his party.

_____

_____

giraffes
elephants
penguins
tigers

4. Tell what animals we saw at the zoo.

_____

_____

Use Commas in a List

Answer each question with a sentence that has three or more things in a list. Use commas to separate the items.

1. What foods do you like?

_____

_____

2. What are your favorite sports?

_____

_____

3. What games do you like to play?

_____

_____

4. Who are some of your friends?

_____

_____

Commas are used in dates and addresses.

- Use a **comma** between the day and the year in a date.

July 4, 1776

October 25, 1946

January 1, 2002

- Use a **comma** between the city and state, province, or country in an address.

Monterey, California

Norman, Oklahoma

New Brunswick, Nova Scotia

Ottawa, Ontario

Paris, France

Comma Usage

Write the Dates

Rule
20

Use a calendar to write the date for each holiday this year.

1. New Year's Day is the first
day of the year.

_____

2. Martin Luther King, Jr. Day is
the third Monday in January.

_____

3. Presidents' Day is the third
Monday in February.

_____

4. Valentine's Day is the
fourteenth day of February.

_____

5. Mother's Day is the second
Sunday in May.

_____

6. Memorial Day is the last
Monday in May.

_____

7. Father's Day is the third
Sunday in June.

_____

8. Labor Day is the first Monday
in September.

_____

9. Veterans Day is the eleventh
day of the eleventh month.

_____

10. Thanksgiving Day is the fourth
Thursday in November.

_____

Commas in an Address

A Write your address. Use a comma between the city and the state.

_____

_____

_____

B Write a friend's address here. Don't forget the comma.

_____

_____

_____

What and When

Answer the questions. Use commas between the day and year and the city and state.

1. When is your birthday this year?

_____

2. What is the address of your school?

_____

_____

_____

3. When is your best friend's birthday this year?

_____

4. What is the capital city and name of your state?

_____

5. What date is your favorite holiday this year?

_____

Rule 21

Apostrophes (') are used to show belonging.

- Add an apostrophe (') and **s** to show that something belongs to one person.

    Bob**'s** bicycle

    Mr. Smith**'s** lunch

    the dog**'s** bone

    James**'s** bicycle

- When a word showing more than one thing ends in an **s**, just add an apostrophe (') to show belonging.

    girls—girl**s'** bicycles   boys—boy**s'** bathroom

    dogs—dog**s'** bones   bunnies—bunnie**s'** ears

Possessive Nouns

Grammar and Punctuation, Grade 2 • EMC 2712

Which Is Correct?

Circle the correct word to complete the sentence.

1. That is (Bob's   Bobs) book.

2. Those are (Jennys   Jenny's) pencils.

3. That is Mr. (Bells   Bell's) science kit.

4. Our class played at our (city's   citys) park.

5. (Mikes   Mike's) house is next to mine.

6. That is our (school's   schools) flagpole.

7. The (dolls   doll's) hair is blond.

8. My (dog's   dogs) tail is short.

9. The (cats   cat's) fur is white and black.

10. The (boys   boy's) tree house is finally finished.

Name _____

Show Possession

Read the sentences. Write a word to show who owns what.

1. The jump ropes belong to the girls.

the _____ jump ropes

2. The tools belong to the workers.

the _____ tools

3. The paintings belong to the art students.

the _____ paintings

4. The cars belong to the parents.

the _____ cars

5. The bones belong to the dogs.

the _____ bones

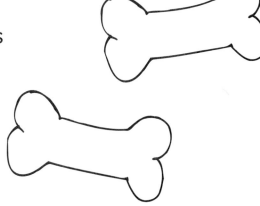
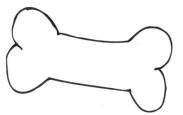

Whose Is It?

Write a complete sentence to answer each question. Use words with an **'s** to show possession.

1. Whose pencil is this?

_____

2. Whose shoes are those?

_____

3. Whose bike is that?

_____

4. Whose toys are these?

_____

5. Whose hat is this?

_____

6. Whose skates are those?

_____

Add **ed** to most action words to tell that something has already happened.

They cook**ed** dinner for the whole family.

The dog bark**ed** at the cat.

Alice jump**ed** rope with her sister.

Past Tense

Name _____

Add the Ending

Add **ed** to each verb. Then write a sentence using the new word.

1. walk _____

_____

2. pick _____

_____

3. answer _____

_____

4. listen _____

_____

5. bark _____

_____

6. crawl _____

_____

What Happened?

Read each sentence. Draw a line under the verb. Rewrite the sentence to show that it happened in the past.

I <u>watch</u> my favorite movie.   I **watched** my favorite movie.

1. I talk on the telephone.

_____

2. I walk to school.

_____

3. I kick the ball.

_____

4. I look for my lost sock.

_____

5. I play with my puppy.

_____

                   Grammar and Punctuation, Grade 2 • EMC 2712

At the Park

Change the word to tell that it happened in the past.

1. I _____ the back door.
   open

2. I _____ my dog, Sparky.
   call

3. We _____ to the park together.
   walk

4. Sparky _____ with a tennis ball.
   play

5. I _____ for my friends.
   look

6. Sparky _____ up and down.
   jump

7. We _____ at Sparky.
   laugh

8. It _____ to rain.
   start

9. Mother _____ us up in the car.
   pick

Some words change before an ending is added.

- Change **y** to **i** and add **es**.

  baby   bab**ies**

  hobb**y**   hobb**ies**

- Drop the **e** and add **ing** or **ed**.

  rid**e**   rid**ing**

  sav**e**   sav**ed**

- Double the final consonant and add **ed** or **ing**.

  cu**t**   cu**tting**

  sto**p**   sto**pped**

Adding Endings

Change y to i

Change **y** to **i** and add **es** to show more than one.

One	More Than One
1. lady	_____
2. baby	_____
3. daisy	_____
4. body	_____
5. pony	_____
6. bunny	_____
7. puppy	_____
8. city	_____
9. penny	_____
10. candy	_____

Drop the Silent e

A Add **ing** and **ed** to the words below. Remember to drop the **e** first.

Add **ing**	Add **ed**

1. dive _____

2. ride _____

3. give _____

4. write _____

5. use _____

6. face _____

7. pile _____

8. joke _____

9. smile _____

10. dance _____

B Write a sentence using these new words.

1. giving

_____

_____

2. joked

_____

_____

Double the Final Consonant

A Double the final consonant and add **ed** or **ing**.

Add **ed**	Add **ing**

1. slip _____

2. clap _____

3. flop _____

4. mop _____

5. grin _____

6. drip _____

7. hit _____

8. flap _____

9. stop _____

10. dig _____

B Write the correct word in each sentence.

1. The children _____ after Jared sang.

2. The rooster was _____ its wings.

3. Tammy was _____ in the sand.

4. The girls _____ at the boys.

Some special words show that something happened in the past.

- is—**was**

  Today is Monday.
  Yesterday **was** Sunday.

- has—**had**

  He has milk for lunch.
  Yesterday he **had** juice.

- do—**did**

  Do you have time to play?
  Did you play yesterday?

- sing—**sang**

  We sing every day.
  Yesterday we **sang** songs.

- eat—**ate**

  Do you want to eat this apple?
  I **ate** one already.

- drink—**drank**

  Drink your milk.
  I **drank** it already.

- leave—**left**

  When did they leave?
  They **left** an hour ago.

- go—**went**

  Let's go to the park.
  I **went** there this morning.

- ring—**rang**

  Did you hear the bell ring?
  It **rang** loudly.

- buy—**bought**

  We buy milk at that store.
  We **bought** some on Monday.

Irregular Verbs

Special Verbs

Read each sentence. Draw a line under the verb. Rewrite the sentence to show that it happened in the past.

Tammy <u>eats</u> breakfast.   Tammy **ate** breakfast.

1. Tammy drinks her milk.

_____

2. The telephone rings.

_____

3. Tammy leaves her house.

_____

4. Tammy goes to school.

_____

5. Tammy buys her lunch.

_____

Match the Verbs

Draw a line to match each word with the word that shows what happened in the past.

is	sang
drink	did
run	was
sing	went
go	drank
has	ate
do	ran
eat	had
buy	rang
ring	bought

Today and Yesterday

Fill in the blanks.

1. Today I run.   Yesterday I _____.

2. Today I sing.   Yesterday I _____.

3. Today I go.   Yesterday I _____.

4. Today I eat.   Yesterday I _____.

5. Today I buy.   Yesterday I _____.

6. Today I leave.   Yesterday I _____.

7. Today I have.   Yesterday I _____.

8. Today I drink.   Yesterday I _____.

Rule 25

The endings **er** and **est** are used to compare things.

• Use **er** to compare two things.

The tree is tall**er** than the swing.

Hand me the long**er** of the two pencils.

The soccer ball is bigg**er** than the baseball.

• Use **est** to compare three or more things.

She is the thinn**est** of the four girls.

Brandon is the tall**est** boy in the class.

I think that is the pretti**est** painting in the museum.

Comparative & Superlative

Name _____

Compare Two Things

Write three sentences comparing these two cats. Use comparing words that end in **er**.

1. _____

_____

2. _____

_____

3. _____

_____

Compare More Than Two Things

Write a sentence to compare the three things in each box. Be sure to use a word that ends in **est**.

_____

_____

_____

_____

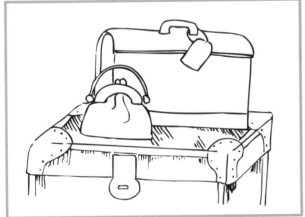

_____

_____

_____

_____

         Grammar and Punctuation, Grade 2 • EMC 2712

Draw Pictures

Draw pictures to show the meaning of these comparing words.

long	longer

big	bigger

tall	taller	tallest

small	smaller	smallest

Notes to the Teacher

Rule 1, Page 3

To avoid confusion at this level, this rule was simplified.

A sentence usually names something or someone and tells what that something or someone is or does. In an imperative sentence (one that gives a command), the subject *you* is understood. For example:

Stop!

Come with me.

Pass the butter, please.

Grammar and Punctuation Review
Part A, Rules 1–9

Circle the letter for each correct answer.

A1. Which of these shows the part of a sentence that names something or someone?

A My sister <u>wants a pet rabbit</u>.

B <u>My sister</u> wants a pet rabbit.

A2. Which group of words should begin with a capital letter?

A they play soccer after school.

B on the soccer field behind the school.

A3. Which punctuation mark should go at the end of this sentence?
How many students went on the field trip ____

A period (.)   **B** question mark (?)   **C** exclamation mark (!)

A4. Which words should begin with capital letters?

A neighbor   **B** sarah

A5. **A** elementary school   **B** mount rushmore

A6. **A** april   **B** holiday

A7. Which word names a person, place, or thing?

A lake   **B** swim

A8. Which word describes a cat?

A play   **B** white

A9. Which word describes an action?

A kick   **B** ball

Grammar and Punctuation Review
Part B, Rules 10–17

Circle the letter for each correct answer.

B1. Which two words can be put together to make a new word?

A butter cookie   **B** butter cube   **C** butter fly

B2. Which contraction can be made from the words **I have**?

A I'd   **B** I'm   **C** I've

B3. Which word can take the place of the underlined word?

<u>Carlos</u> ate a sandwich.

A He   **B** Him

Which word should go in each blank?

B4. Ryan gave _____ a book to read.

A I   **B** me

B5. _____ mailed a letter to Grandmother.

A Us   **B** We

B6. What are _____ going to bring for a snack?

A them   **B** they

B7. Which word means more than one boy?

A boys   **B** boyes

B8. Which word means more than one foot?

A feet   **B** foots

Grammar and Punctuation Review
Part C, Rules 18–25

Circle the letter for each correct answer.

Which word should go in the blank?

C1. They _____ singing a song.

A is   **B** are

C2. Which sentence uses commas correctly?

A Please bring pencils, paper and, an eraser.

B Please bring, pencils, paper, and, an eraser.

C Please bring pencils, paper, and an eraser.

C3. **A** He lives in Salem, Oregon.

B He lives on Washington, Street.

C He lives in New York, City.

Which word should go in each blank?

C4. Here is _____ library card.

A Jill's   **B** Jills'

C5. He _____ for the school bus.

A wait   **B** waited

C6. They _____ to rest under a tree.

A stoped   **B** stopped

C7. She _____ a present for her baby brother.

A buy   **B** bought

C8. That was the _____ movie I have ever seen.

A long   **B** longer   **C** longest

         Grammar and Punctuation, Grade 2 • EMC 2712

Name

Rule	Skill	Activity Pages			Review Questions		
		Circle when completed			Number	Correct	Not Correct
1	Identify the two parts of a sentence.	4	5	6	A1		
2	Capitalize the first word in sentences.	8	9	10	A2		
3	End sentences with correct punctuation.	12	13	14	A3		
4	Capitalize the names of people and pets.	16	17	18	A4		
5	Capitalize the names of specific places.	20	21	22	A5		
6	Capitalize the names of days, months, holidays.	24	25	26	A6		
7	Identify nouns.	28	29	30	A7		
8	Identify adjectives.	32	33	34	A8		
9	Identify verbs.	36	37	38	A9		
10	Identify compound words.	40	41	42	B1		
11	Identify contractions.	44	45	46	B2		
12	Identify pronouns.	48	49	50	B3		
13	Use the words *I* and *me*.	52	53	54	B4		
14	Use the words *we* and *us*.	56	57	58	B5		
15	Use the words *they* and *them*.	60	61	62	B6		
16	Add *s* or *es* to make a noun plural.	64	65	66	B7		
17	Identify irregular plural nouns.	68	69	70	B8		
18	Use the words *is* and *are*.	72	73	74	C1		
19	Use commas to separate things in a list.	76	77	78	C2		
20	Use commas in dates and addresses.	80	81	82	C3		
21	Use apostrophes in possessive nouns.	84	85	86	C4		
22	Add *ed* to form past tense verbs.	88	89	90	C5		
23	Add endings to nouns and verbs.	92	93	94	C6		
24	Identify irregular past tense verbs.	96	97	98	C7		
25	Use comparative & superlative words.	100	101	102	C8		

Answer Key

Page 4
Items 2, 3, 5, and 8 should be circled.
Items 1, 4, 6, and 7 should be crossed out.

Page 5
1. (Nick) rode his new blue bike.
2. (Susie and Toshi) played with the dollhouse.
3. (The two girls) jumped up and down.
4. (Becky and her grandmother) played in the snow.
5. (Jonathan) flew his paper airplane.
6. (Mrs. Smith's class) walked to the lunchroom.
7. (Each boy) read two books.
8. (Isabel) won the race.
9. (Mom and Dad) went to the store.

Page 6
Names something or someone
Two big dogs
Jane and Tamara
Cindy and Daniel

Tells what it is or does
raced down the street.
rode their bikes.
played checkers.

Page 8
1. The   6. There
3. Then   8. The
4. There

Sentences will vary. Check for proper capitalization.

Page 9
1. My pet lives in a cage.
2. It can talk and squawk.
3. My pet has a beak.
4. It has green and yellow feathers.

Drawings will vary.

Page 10
1. I   5. E
2. I   6. M
3. M   7. S
4. S   8. W

Page 12
Period (.)
Pizza is my favorite food
I like a lot of cheese on mine
Many toppings can go on a pizza

Question Mark (?)
What is your favorite kind
Do you like pepperoni on it
Which toppings do you like

Page 13
1. .   5. ?
2. !   6. !
3. .   7. .
4. crossed out

Page 14
1. ?   6. .
2. .   7. ?
3. !   8. !
4. .   9. . OR !
5. .   10. ?

Page 16
1. Mark
2. Midnight
3. Baby
4. Baby, Midnight
5. Midnight
6. Baby, Midnight
7. (no change)
8. Baby
9. Midnight

Page 17
Answers will vary. Check for proper capitalization.

Page 18
1. Kristen, Ronnie
2. Socks
3. Mrs. Gonzalez
4. Dr. Hopkins
5. Karl, Rover
6. Mr. Lee

Page 20
1. Rocky Mountain National Park
2. Colby
3. Sweet Pea, Blossom
4. Denver
5. Leonard, Sunset Beach

Answers will vary. Check for proper capitalization.

Page 21
Answers will vary. Check for proper capitalization.

Page 22
1. Disneyland
2. Los Angeles
3. Yosemite National Park
4. Mount Rushmore
5. Colonial Williamsburg
6. Carlsbad Caverns
7. Mississippi River
8. Cape Cod

Page 24
1. Monday   4. Tuesday
2. Wednesday 5. Sunday
3. Friday   6. Saturday

Answers will vary. Check for proper capitalization.

Page 25
January, February, March, April, May, June, July, August, September, October, November, December

Page 26
1. We plan to watch the fireworks on Independence Day.
2. The class drew leprechauns for St. Patrick's Day.
3. Michael's birthday is on Father's Day this year.
4. Did you hunt for eggs on Easter?
5. Mrs. Smith's class learned about Chinese New Year.

Page 26 (continued)
6. Tenisha's family had a party during Kwanzaa.
7. We roasted a big turkey for Thanksgiving.
8. Did you make Mother a card for Valentine's Day?

Page 28
Zip lay down under the tree. A little bee buzzed near his ear. Zip flipped his tail at the bee and rolled over in the grass. It was a quiet day. The family had gone to the beach. The house was empty. The sun was warm. Zip yawned. Soon Zip was dreaming of a yummy bone.

Zip is a dog.

Page 29
person: teacher, boy, girl
place: school, playground, library
thing: book, jump rope, pencil

Answers will vary. Check for proper capitalization.

Page 30
Answers will vary.

Page 32
1. fluffy, yellow, round
2. big, green
3. tiny, silver, clear
4. flat, white
5. green, leafy
6. gray, toy

Answers will vary.

Page 33
Answers will vary.

Page 34
1. funny, 1
2. fast, quick, 2
3. two, silly, 2
4. big, funny, colorful, 3
5. large, red, 2
6. gigantic, yellow 2

Page 34 (continued)
7. silly, loud, green, 3
8. quick, 1

Page 36
1. planted
2. warmed
3. watered
4. poked
5. grew, grew
6. was
7. appeared
8. picked
9. ate

Page 37
Answers will vary.

Page 38
Answers will vary.

Page 40
1. mailbox, mail, box
2. sandbox, sand, box
3. baseball, base, ball
4. seashells, sea, shells
5. playground, play, ground

Page 41
downhill
notebook
into
baseball
shoelace
doorknob

Page 42
1. butterfly
2. sunflower
3. cupcake
4. skateboard
5. cowboy
6. doghouse

Page 44
1. o
2. woul
3. o
4. i
5. wi
6. a
7. o
8. ha

Sentences will vary.

Page 45
1. haven't
2. don't
3. wouldn't
4. isn't
5. didn't
6. couldn't
7. weren't
8. aren't
9. can't
10. doesn't

Page 46
1. you're
2. we're
3. he's
4. I'd
5. that's
6. she's
7. it's
8. I'll
9. I'm
10. let's

I am — I'm
has not — hasn't
are not — aren't
she will — she'll
have not — haven't
I will — I'll
she is — she's

Page 48
1. He hit a home run.
2. She drives a school bus.
3. I couldn't wait to see it.
4. I invited him to my birthday party.
5. She waved to him from the bus.
6. It was the biggest thing he had ever seen.

Page 49
Donna and I are good friends. We love to play games and read books. We like to play checkers and dominoes. They are terrific games to play. When we are outside, we like to play soccer or baseball. Donna is a good kicker, but I am a great hitter. We also love to read books. Charlotte's Web is my favorite. It is a wonderful story. Donna likes it, too.

Page 50
1. It is falling.
2. We want to play outside.
3. He put on his snowsuit.
4. She put on some boots.
5. He grabbed his jacket.
6. They got out the sled.
7. We dashed outside.
8. It was terrific!

Page 52

1. I	5. I
2. me	6. me
3. I	7. me
4. I	8. I

Page 53

1. I	5. me
2. me	6. I
3. I	7. me
4. me	8. I

Page 54

You are doing something

I like to play baseball.
Sam and I are reading.
I went to the store.

Something happens to you

Kelly handed me the paper.
Marta worked with me.
Please give me the ball.

Page 56

Answers will vary. Check for proper use of **we** and **us**.

Page 57

1. We	5. We
2. us	6. us
3. us	7. us
4. we	8. We

Page 58

You and others do something

We went to the playground.
We played basketball.
At school we learn new things.

Something happens to you and others

Dad took us to the game.
Carla read a book to us.
Mom gave us some drinks.

Page 60

1. They take cooking lessons.
2. Yesterday they joined the class.
3. They made a fruit salad.
4. Then they ate it.
5. They washed the dishes.

Page 61

Tony, Elise, and Sam wanted to plan a class party. <u>They</u> asked Mrs. Supino for permission. Mrs. Supino told <u>them</u> that it was okay. <u>They</u> planned games and made snacks. The class loved it. All of the students thanked <u>them</u> for planning the party.

Last month Robin's dog had puppies. <u>They</u> were so tiny. The mother dog took good care of <u>them</u>. Now <u>they</u> are running around. Robin likes to play with <u>them</u>. Then <u>they</u> fall asleep on her lap. <u>They</u> are so cute!

Page 62

Several people do something

They ran to the swings.
They played with Tina.
Later they went to the park.

Something happens to several people

Chaz asked them to help.
Jamal worked with them.
Pedro tossed the ball to them.

Page 64

1. shoes	5. bike
2. hat	6. team
3. dog	7. dishes
4. box	8. buses

Page 65

1. stamp, 1, stamps, 1
2. dish, 1, dishes, 2
3. dog, 1, dogs, 1
4. sandwich, 2, sandwiches, 3
5. cupcake, 2, cupcakes, 2
6. bench, 1, benches, 2
7. frog, 1, frogs, 1
8. fox, 1, foxes, 2

Page 66

1. s	7. s
2. s	8. es
3. es	9. s
4. s	10. s
5. s	11. s
6. es	12. s

Page 68

children, man, mouse, men, child, mice

1. mice
2. child
3. men
4. children

Page 69

(picture of children) — children
(picture of child) — child
(picture of tooth) — tooth
(picture of teeth) — teeth
(picture of goose) — goose
(picture of geese) — geese
(picture of foot) — foot
(picture of feet) — feet

Page 70

1. child	6. women
2. goose	7. geese
3. tooth	8. foot
4. feet	9. teeth
5. children	10. woman

Page 72

1. are	6. is
2. are	7. is
3. is	8. are
4. is	9. are
5. is	10. are

Page 73

1. is	6. is
2. is	7. is
3. are	8. is
4. are	9. are
5. is	10. are

Page 74

1. are	5. is
2. is	6. are
3. are	7. is
4. is	8. is

Answers will vary. Check for proper use of **is** and **are**.

Page 76
1. He bought nails, screws, and wood to build his doghouse.
2. We bought oranges, apples, pears, and bananas at the grocery store.
3. Mike asked Tory, Cassie, Jake, Jared, and Jesse to the party.
4. I have sheets, blankets, and a bedspread on my bed.
5. We took books, games, magazines, and puzzles on our trip.
6. The Scouts will need backpacks, sleeping bags, clothes, and food for camp.
7. We used pink, purple, and silver paint in LaDonna's bedroom.
8. My favorite sandwich has peanut butter, honey, and bananas on it.

Answers will vary. Check for proper use of commas.

Page 77
1. Tom packed a raincoat, compass, flashlight, and water bottle for his camping trip.
2. Jolynn had peach yogurt, string cheese, carrots, and chocolate milk in her lunch.
3. Andrew is inviting Thomas, Chris, Todd, and Lee to his party.
4. We saw giraffes, elephants, penguins, and tigers at the zoo.

Page 78
Answers will vary. Check for proper use of commas in a list.

Page 80
Answers will vary. Check for proper use of commas between the day and year.

Page 81
Answers will vary. Check for proper use of commas between the city and state.

Page 82
Answers will vary. Check for proper use of commas.

Page 84
1. Bob's
2. Jenny's
3. Bell's
4. city's
5. Mike's
6. school's
7. doll's
8. dog's
9. cat's
10. boy's

Page 85
1. girls'
2. workers'
3. students'
4. parents'
5. dogs'

Page 86
Answers will vary. Check for proper use of **'s** as a possessive.

Page 88
1. walked
2. picked
3. answered
4. listened
5. barked
6. crawled

Sentences will vary.

Page 89
1. I talked on the telephone.
2. I walked to school.
3. I kicked the ball.
4. I looked for my lost sock.
5. I played with my puppy.

Page 90
1. opened
2. called
3. walked
4. played
5. looked
6. jumped
7. laughed
8. started
9. picked

Page 92
1. ladies
2. babies
3. daisies
4. bodies
5. ponies
6. bunnies
7. puppies
8. cities
9. pennies
10. candies

Page 93
Add ing
1. diving
2. riding
3. giving
4. writing
5. using

Add ed
6. faced
7. piled
8. joked
9. smiled
10. danced

Sentences will vary.

Page 94
Add ed
1. slipped
2. clapped
3. flopped
4. mopped
5. grinned

Add ing
6. dripping
7. hitting
8. flapping
9. stopping
10. digging

1. clapped
2. flapping
3. digging
4. grinned

Page 96
1. Tammy <u>drinks</u> her milk. Tammy drank her milk.
2. The telephone <u>rings</u>. The telephone rang.
3. Tammy <u>leaves</u> her house. Tammy left her house.
4. Tammy <u>goes</u> to school. Tammy went to school.
5. Tammy <u>buys</u> her lunch. Tammy bought her lunch.

Page 97

Page 98
1. ran
2. sang
3. went
4. ate
5. bought
6. left
7. had
8. drank

Page 100
Answers will vary. Check for comparing words ending with **er**.

Page 101
Answers will vary. Check for comparing words ending with **er** and **est**.

Page 102
Pictures will vary. Check for correct meaning of the comparing words.

Grammar and Punctuation Review

Part A
A1. B
A2. A
A3. B
A4. B
A5. B
A6. A
A7. A
A8. B
A9. A

Part B
B1. C
B2. C
B3. A
B4. B
B5. B
B6. B
B7. A
B8. A

Part C
C1. B
C2. C
C3. A
C4. A
C5. B
C6. B
C7. B
C8. C